*The Joys
of Friendship*

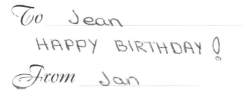

To Jean
HAPPY BIRTHDAY!
From Jan

*Y*es, we must ever be friends;
and of all who offer you friendship,
let me be ever the first, the truest,
the nearest and dearest!

HENRY WADSWORTH LONGFELLOW

A kind heart is a fountain of
gladness, making everything in
its vicinity freshen into smiles.

WASHINGTON IRVING

$\mathcal{W}$e cannot tell the precise moment when a friendship starts. It is like filling a vessel drop-by-drop which makes it at last run over; so in a series of kindnesses there is at last one which makes the heart run over.

JAMES BOSWELL

*M*ay you always find three
welcomes in life,
In a garden during summer,
At a fireside during winter,
And whatever the day or season,
In the kind eyes of a friend.

*F*riendship is not won by the giving of things, but by the giving of the heart.

ROY LESSIN

A friend loves at all times.

PROVERBS 17:17 NKJV

*Y*our only treasures are those which you carry in your heart.

DEMOPHILUS

*T*hose who bring sunshine to the lives of others cannot keep it from themselves.

SIR JAMES M. BARRIE

*F*riendship is a sheltering tree;
Oh, the joys that come down
shower-like!

SAMUEL TAYLOR COLERIDGE

*B*lessed are they who have the gift of making friends, for it is one of God's best gifts.

THOMAS HUGHES

To have a friend is to have one of the sweetest gifts that life can bring; to be a friend is to have a solemn and tender education of soul from day to day.

AMY ROBERTSON BROWN

A friend is the hope of the heart.

RALPH WALDO EMERSON

Those who are loving and kind show that they are the children of God.

1 JOHN 4:7 TLB

$\mathcal{I}$ thank you, God in heaven, for friends. When morning wakes, when daytime ends, I have the consciousness of loving hands that touch my own, of tender glance and gentle tone, of thoughts that cheer and bless!

MARGARET SANGSTER

$\mathcal{I}$'m so glad you are here....
It helps me to realize how
beautiful my world is.

RAINER MARIA RILKE

$\mathcal{B}$e of one mind, live in peace;
and the God of peace shall be
with you.

2 CORINTHIANS 13:11 KJV

$\mathcal{W}$e are so very rich if we know just a few
people in a way in which we know no others.

CATHERINE BRAMWELL-BOOTH

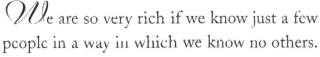

To know someone here or there with whom you feel there is an understanding in spite of distances or thoughts unexpressed—that can make of this earth a garden.

GOETHE

True friends, like ivy
  and the wall,
Both stand together,
  and together fall.

A friend is a person with whom I may be sincere, before whom I may think out loud.

RALPH WALDO EMERSON

*F*ew delights can equal the mere presence of one whom we trust utterly.

GEORGE MACDONALD

*F*riendship is love with understanding.

ANCIENT PROVERB

*O*ur road will be smooth
    and untroubled
no matter what care life may send;
If we travel the pathway together,
and walk side by side with a friend.

A mile walked with a friend
contains only a hundred steps.

Russian Proverb

*F*riends...they cherish each other's hopes. They are kind to each other's dreams.

HENRY DAVID THOREAU

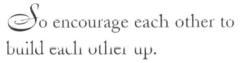

*S*o encourage each other to build each other up.

1 THESSALONIANS 5:11 TLB

A friend is what the heart needs all the time.

HENRY VAN DYKE

It is my friends that have made the story of my life. In a thousand ways they have turned my limitations into beautiful privileges, and enabled me to walk serene and happy in the shadow cast by my deprivation.

HELEN KELLER

$\mathcal{I}$ thank God far more for friends than for my daily bread—for friendship is the bread of the heart.

MARY MITFORD

$\mathcal{T}$here is in friendship something of all relations, and something above them all. It is the golden thread that ties the hearts of all the world.

JOHN EVELYN

Friendship is a
cadence of divine melody
melting through the heart.
MILDMAY

When hands reach out in
friendship, hearts are touched
with joy.

All our actions take their hue
from the complexion of the heart.
FRANCIS BACON

$\mathcal{I}$t is only with the heart that one can see rightly.

ANTOINE DE SAINT-EXUPÉRY

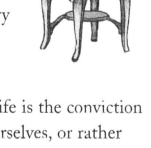

$\mathcal{I}$ thank my God upon every remembrance of you.

PHILIPPIANS 1:3 KJV

$\mathcal{T}$he supreme happiness of life is the conviction that we are loved, loved for ourselves, or rather loved in spite of ourselves.

VICTOR HUGO

*W*hat wisdom can you find that is greater than kindness?

JEAN JACQUES ROUSSEAU

*T*he secret of life is that all we have and are is a gift of grace to be shared.

LLOYD JOHN OGILVIE

*G*ive generously, for your gifts will return to you later.

ECCLESIASTES 11:1 TLB

*K*ind words are jewels that live in
the heart and soul and remain as
blessed memories.

<small>MARVEA JOHNSON</small>

*W*hat the dew is to the flower,
Gentle words are to the soul.

<small>POLLY RUPE</small>

I breathed a song into the air,
it fell to earth I know not where....
And the song, from beginning to end,
I found again in the heart of a friend.

HENRY WADSWORTH LONGFELLOW

*T*he language of friendship is not
words but meaning.

*O*h, the comfort, the inexpressible comfort, of feeling safe with a person; having neither to weigh thoughts nor measure words, but to pour them all out just as they are.

GEORGE ELIOT

*B*e...full of sympathy toward each other, loving one another with tender hearts and humble minds.

1 PETER 3:8 TLB

*T*here's something beautiful about finding
one's innermost thoughts in another.

OLIVER SCHREINER

*F*riends will not only live
in harmony, but in melody.

HENRY DAVID THOREAU

*L*et not the grass grow on
the path of friendship.

NATIVE AMIRICAN PROVERB

As gold more splendid
   from the fire appears,
Thus friendship brightens
   by the length of years.

OVID

A friend is one who joyfully sings
with you when you are on the
mountain top, and silently
walks beside you through
the valley.

WILLIAM A. WARD

May the road
rise to meet you,
May the wind be always
at your back,
May the sun shine warm
upon your face,
May the rain fall soft
upon your fields,
And, until we meet again,
May God hold you in the
palm of his hand.

IRISH BLESSING

*F*riendship is precious, not only in the shade, but in the sunshine of life.

*W*hen others are happy, be happy with them. If they are sad, share their sorrow.

ROMANS 12:15 TLB

*T*he sun shines not on us but in us.

JOHN MUIR

$\mathcal{A}$ friend is one to whom one may pour out all the contents of one's heart, chaff and grain together, knowing that gentle hands will take and sift it, keep what is worth keeping, and with a breath of kindness, blow the rest away.

GEORGE ELIOT

*S*ee to it that you really do love each other warmly, with all your hearts.

1 PETER 1:22 TLB

*W*e must love our friends as true amateurs love paintings; they have their eyes perpetually fixed on the fine parts, and see no others.

MADAME D'ÉPINAY

A knowledge that another has felt as we have felt, and seen things not much otherwise than we have seen them, will continue to the end to be one of life's choicest blessings.

ROBERT LOUIS STEVENSON

A true friend is a gift of God... and only he who made hearts can unite them.

*P*ut on a heart of compassion,
kindness, humility, gentleness,
and patience.

COLOSSIANS 3:12 NASB

*F*riendship is like love at its
best: not blind but sympathetically
all-seeing; a support which does not wait for
understanding; an act of faith which does not
need, but always has, reason.

LOUIS UNTERMEYER

*O*ne friend ever watches and cares for another.
RANDLE COSGRAVE

*M*y friends are an oasis to me, encouraging me to go on. They arc essential to my well-being.
DEE BRESTIN

*M*ercy is as beautiful in a time of trouble as rain clouds in a time of drought.
ECCLESIASTICUS

$\mathcal{I}$ wish you love and strength and faith
    and wisdom,
Goods, gold enough to help some needy one.
I wish you songs, but also blessed silence,
And God's sweet peace when every day
    is done.

DOROTHY NELL MCDONALD

$\mathcal{T}$he things that matter the
most in this world, they can
never be held in our hand.

GLORIA GAITHER

The true way and
the sure way to friendship is
through humility—being open
to each other, accepting each other
just as we are, knowing each other.

MOTHER TERESA

There is no better exercise for the
heart than reaching down and lifting
up people.

JOHN ANDREW HOLMER

*I*t is always good to know, if only in passing, a charming human being; it refreshes our lives like flowers and wood and clear brooks.

GEORGE ELIOT

*M*ost of all, let love guide your life.

COLOSSIANS 3:14 TLB

$\mathcal{N}$o love, no friendship can cross the path of our destiny without leaving some mark on it forever.

FRANÇOIS MAURIAC

$\mathcal{M}$ay you have warm words
   on a cold evening,
a full moon on a dark night,
and the road downhill
   all the way to your door.

IRISH BLESSING

*F*riendship: Gentle as the dew from silken skies, radiant as some glorious diadem, set with countless stars.

YEOMAN SHIELD

*H*old a true friend with both your hands.

NIGERIAN PROVERB

*W*hen you love someone you will be loyal to him no matter what the cost.

1 CORINTHIANS 13:7 TLB

$\mathcal{N}$ow may the
warming love of friends
Surround you as you go
Down the path of light and
laughter
Where the happy memories grow.

HELEN LOWRIE MARSHALL

$\mathcal{W}$hat a thing friendship is—
World without end!

ROBERT BROWNING